LITTLE PRAYERS

Selected by Esther Wilkin

Illustrated by Eloise Wilkin

A GOLDEN BOOK, New York
Western Publishing Company, Inc.
Racine, Wisconsin 53404

Copyright © 1980, 1975 by Western Publishing Company, Inc.
All rights reserved. Printed in the U.S.A.
No part of this book may be reproduced or copied in any form
without written permission from the publisher.
GOLDEN®, GOLDEN® & DESIGN, A GOLDEN LOOK-LOOK® BOOK,
and A GOLDEN BOOK®
are trademarks of Western Publishing Company, Inc.
Library of Congress Catalog Card Number: 80-50810
ISBN 0-307-11858-4
F G H I J

FOREWORD

Some of our friends worship in ways that are different from ours, for there are many ways of giving honor and glory to God. This book contains new and old prayers from all over the world.

When we pray, we lift our minds and hearts to God who loves us all. Let us all then be united with Him in love: the love of God for us, our love for Him, and our love for one another.

ACKNOWLEDGMENTS. The editor and publisher have made every effort to trace the ownership of all copyrighted material and to secure permission from holders of the copyrights of such material. In the event of any question arising as to the use of any material, the editor and publisher, while expressing regret for inadvertent error, will be pleased to make the necessary corrections in future printings.

Basic Books, Inc., for "A Jewish Prayer" ("Remember Us for Life"), from *Prayer in Judaism* by Bernard Martin, © 1968 by Basic Books, Inc., Publishers, New York.

Harper & Row, Publishers, Inc., for "A Japanese Prayer" ("For Quietness") by Utsomiya San, from *The World at One in Prayer,* edited by Daniel Johnson Fleming. Copyright 1942 by Harper & Row. Reprinted by permission of the publisher.

Alfred A. Knopf, for "Heaven," copyright 1947 by Langston Hughes. Reprinted from *Selected Poems of Langston Hughes* by Langston Hughes.

The Hebrew Publishing Company, for "A Child's Evening Prayer," from *The Jewish Woman and Her Home,* by Hyman S. Goldin.

Peter Pauper Press, for "Talking with one another," from African Proverbs by C. W. Laslau.

Dana W. Briggs, in behalf of Dixie Willson, (deceased) for "Dear God, I Gratefully Bow My Head," by Dixie Willson.

Union of American Hebrew Congregations, for "Grace After Meals," from *Within Thy Hands* by Ilo Orleans.

The Viking Press, Inc., and Macmillan London and Basingstoke for "The Prayer of the Cricket," from *Prayers from the Ark* by Carmen Bernos de Gasztold (translated by Rumer Godden). English text copyright © 1962 by Rumer Godden.

War Resisters League, for "An American Indian Prayer," from the 1974 WRL Peace Calendar, *As Long as the Rivers Shall Flow.*

Bless the Lord

All you things the Lord has made, bless the Lord;
   Give Him glory and praise forever!

Sun and moon, bless the Lord;
   Bless the Lord, you stars of heaven.

Dew and rain, bless the Lord;
   Bless the Lord, you winds.

Frost and cold, bless the Lord;
   Bless the Lord, you ice and snow.

Springs of water, bless the Lord;
   Bless the Lord, you seas and rivers.

Fire and heat, bless the Lord;
   Bless the Lord, all things that grow.

Birds of heaven, bless the Lord;
   Bless the Lord, you animals wild and tame.

All you people, bless the Lord;
   Bless the Lord, you children.

The Book of Daniel (adapted)

Morning Prayers

Now before I run to play,
    Let me not forget to pray
To God who kept me through the night
    And waked me with the morning light.

Help me, Lord, to love Thee more
    Than I ever loved before,
In my work and in my play,
    Be Thou with me through the day.

                  Amen.

Author Unknown

For this new morning and its light,
For rest and shelter of the night,
For health and food, for love and friends,
For every gift Your goodness sends,
    We thank You, gracious Lord.

Anonymous

O Lord, You know how busy
I must be today.
If I forget You,
Do not forget me.

Jacob Astley

A Little Girl Prays

Dear God,
My Dad says
   You want me to love You
   more than I love him...
   or Mommy.
I wondered
   how I could.
I asked my Dad
   about it and he said,
"Well, you love the cookies
   Mommy makes for you.
And you love Mommy
   more than
   you love the cookies.
It is something like that.
You love
   your Mommy and Dad,
   and your Mommy and Dad
   love you.
God gave us to you,
   and He gave you to us.
God gives us all good things.
God loves us.
That is why we love Him
   with all our heart,
   with all our soul,
   with all our strength."
That is what my Dad said.
I do love You, God.
   and thank You. Amen.

E. W.

A Little Boy Prays

Dear God,
My Mommy is always
   telling me to hurry.
It takes me
   a long time
   to put on my socks,
   she says;
And a long time
   to tie my
   shoelaces.
I tell her
   no matter what I'm doing,
   I like to
   think about things.
She hugs me
   and calls me
   her little Snail.
He does Your holy
   will slowly,
   she says.
She wants me
   to do Your will, too,
   but a little bit
   faster
   because I'm a boy.
I'll try, dear God. Amen.

                 E.W.

*The Snail does the Holy
   Will of God slowly.*

        G. K. Chesterton

A Child's Prayer

There's no one awake
   in the world but me
And the robin singing
   in the apple tree.

God bless the robin
And God bless me.

God bless my eyes
And the things I see,
A big blue flower
And a bumble bee.

God bless my ears
And the sounds I hear,
The rustle of leaves
   in the poplar trees
   far and near.

And bless my feet
Wherever I go
   running fast,
   walking slow.

God bless the words
I say today.
Let them be kind
   and friendly.

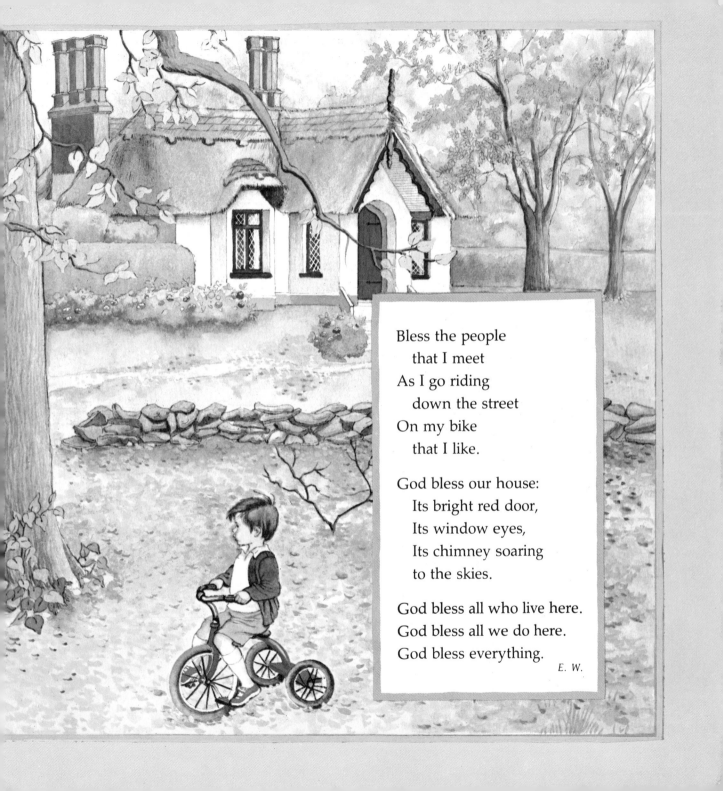

Bless the people
   that I meet
As I go riding
   down the street
On my bike
   that I like.

God bless our house:
   Its bright red door,
   Its window eyes,
   Its chimney soaring
   to the skies.

God bless all who live here.
God bless all we do here.
God bless everything.

E. W.

Dear God,
Be good to me.
The sea is so wide
And my boat is so small.

Prayer of a Breton Fisherman

Praise and gratitude to You, Holy Father,
Who created the skies and heaven first
And after that created the big wet sea
And the heaps of fish in it swimming closely.

An ancient Irish hymn

You must love your neighbor
as yourself.

(The Golden Rule) Romans 13:9

If we have ever been mean to one who loves us,
ever wronged a friend or playmate,
the child next door or a stranger,
O Lord, take away our sin.

The Rig Veda (adapted)

A Buddhist Prayer

When someone is wronged,
he must put aside
all resentment and say,
"My mind shall not be disturbed;
no angry word shall escape my lips;
I will remain kind and friendly,
with loving thoughts
and no secret spite."

A Japanese Prayer

Oh, make my heart so still, so still,
When I am deep in prayer,
That I might hear the white-mist-wreaths
Losing themselves in air.

A Jewish Prayer

Remember us for life,
King who delights in life,
And inscribe us
In the Book of Life
For Your sake,
God of life.

A Christian Prayer

God be in my head
   And in my understanding;
God be in my eyes,
   And in my looking;
God be in my mouth,
   And in my speaking;
God be in my heart,
   And in my thinking;
God be at my end,
   And at my departing.

The Sarum Primer

A Muslim Prayer

I confess there is no God but God,
   I confess there is no God but God.

Grace

For what we are about to receive
May the Lord make us truly thankful.
Amen.

Dear God, I gratefully
bow my head
To thank You
for this daily bread;
And may there be
a goodly share
On every table
everywhere. Amen.

Dixie Willson

Thou art great
And Thou art good,
And we thank Thee
For this food.

Thank You for the world so sweet;
Thank You for the food we eat;
Thank You for the birds that sing;
Thank You, God, for everything!

E. Rutter Leatham

Blessed art Thou,
   O Lord, our King,
Who feedest every
   Living thing;

Who givest bread,
   So that we may
Have strength to do
   Our work each day;

Blessed art Thou,
   For Thou dost give
Food to nourish
   All that live.

Ilo Orleans

Prayers for Little Things

All things bright and beautiful,
  All creatures great and small,
All things wise and wonderful,
  The Lord God made them all.

C.F. Alexander

Dear Father, hear and bless
Thy beasts and singing birds,
And guard with tenderness
Small things that have no words.

Anonymous

He prayeth best who loveth best
All things both great and small,
For the dear God who loveth us
He made and loveth all.

Samuel Taylor Coleridge

O Great Spirit,
Whose voice I hear in the winds,
And whose breath gives life to all the world,
Hear me! I am small and weak, I need your
Strength and wisdom.

Let Me Walk In Beauty, and make my eyes
ever behold the red and purple sunset.

Make My Hands respect the things you have
made and my ears sharp to hear your voice.

Make Me Wise so that I may understand the
things you have taught my people.

Let Me Learn the Lessons you have hidden in
every leaf and rock.

I Seek Strength, not to be greater than my
brother, but to fight my greatest enemy—
myself.

American Indian Prayer

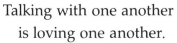

Talking with one another
is loving one another.

African Proverb

Heaven is
The place where
Happiness is
Everywhere.
Animals
And birds sing—
As does
Everything.
To each stone,
"How-do-you-do?"
"Well!! And you?"

Langston Hughes

Prayer for the Burial of a Bird

This sparrow died today, O Lord,
Your feathered creature small.
We lay him in the friendly earth
And ask Your blessing on us all.

E.W.

There are three ways children express sorrow:
Some children cry, some children are silent;
Wise children know how to turn sorrow into song.

Hassidic Writings (adapted)

The Prayer of the Cricket

O God,
I am little and very black
but I thank You
for having shed
Your warm sun
and the quivering
of Your golden corn
on my humble life.

Carmen Bernos de Gasztold (adapted)

(translated by Rumer Godden)

Evening Prayers

Praised be Thou, O Lord our God, Father of all,
    for giving us the sweet rest of the night.
In peace do I lay me down to sleep,
    and may it be Thy will, O Lord,
    that I awake in peace.
I am in the care of the Lord
    when I sleep and when I wake.
In Thy help I trust, O Lord.

from "The Jewish Woman and Her Home"
by Hyman E. Goldin

I see the moon,
    And the moon sees me;
God bless the moon,
    And God bless me.

Father, keep me safe tonight.
Bless Thy child again.
Help me always do the right.
In Christ's name, Amen.

Frederick Hill Meserve

Jesus, Tender Shepherd, Hear Me

Jesus, tender Shepherd, hear me;
Bless Thy little lamb tonight;
Through the darkness be Thou near me,
Watch my sleep till morning light.

All this day Thy hand has led me,
And I thank Thee for Thy care;
Thou has warmed and clothed and fed me;
Listen to my evening prayer.

Mary L. Duncan